THEY'VE GOT IT ALL WRONG!

THE GOSPEL CRISIS

DR CHARLES VOGAN

ISBN 978-1530328031

Ravenbrook Publishers

A subsidiary of
Shenandoah Bible Ministries

www.Ravenbrook.org

www.Shenbible.org

THEY'VE GOT IT ALL WRONG!

THE GOSPEL CRISIS

The Gospel has been changed in modern times.

Our preachers and teachers in the Church are pretty much unanimous on what the Gospel is, and they almost all teach it the same way. But what's alarming is that the modern way of preaching the Gospel *doesn't match up with the way the Apostles preached it.* It's easy to contrast the two by seeing them side-by-side on paper. What that means is that our generation has closed the Bible and come up with a new way of presenting the Gospel.

And for some strange reason, nobody has been checking on what our preachers are doing. Evidently everyone is OK with a new Gospel that "fits in" with our modern generation and its "special needs." It doesn't seem to occur to anybody to check the Bible to see if we have it right.

This is serious. It means we're not in fact the heirs of the Apostles; we no longer have a spiritual connection with the Early Church. And it also means that the power of the Gospel isn't driving our spiritual life within our churches.

> For I am not ashamed of the Gospel, for it is the power of God for salvation to everyone who believes, to the Jew first and also to the Greek. For in it the righteousness of God is revealed from faith for faith, as it is written, "The righteous shall live by faith." (Romans 1:16-17)

3

Why aren't we Biblical anymore?

As responsible Christians, we're supposed to check everything we do against the Scriptures. We are heirs and descendants of our spiritual Fathers; as wise sons, we are to learn from our elders and emulate their faith. We have *not* been given permission to change the message they handed down to us in any way. Jesus very plainly said that *his* words give spiritual life to the children of God. "The words that I have spoken to you are spirit and life." (John 6:63) Peter could see the importance of preserving Christ's words: "*You* have the words of eternal life." (John 6:68)

Why, then, has the modern Church strayed so far from the Apostolic message? Why do our preachers and teachers think it's OK to pull words and even whole verses completely out of context? Why do they casually dismiss the very material that the Apostles considered so essential for presenting the Gospel correctly? We're going to look at some plain proofs that they actually have been doing this very thing.

It's easy to criticize the leaders of the Church; there's always someone who doesn't like the way things are done and they think they know more than the preacher does about how to run the Church. Leaders are natural targets, and often unfairly so.

On the other hand, leaders are not perfect. They have their sins too. There are times when the sheep suddenly realize that they're starving on the "wood, hay and stubble" that they're getting from the Church's ministry. The answer is not simply to accept whatever the leaders do *because* they're leaders, but to accept their leadership *only as they follow Christ.* (1 Corinthians 11:1) But in order to determine that, one has to find out what Christ taught – and that means opening the Bible and taking careful notes. Leaders who are genuinely concerned with the welfare of their flock should have no reason to worry about such followers.

Now the Bereans were of more noble character than the Thessalonians, for they received the message with great eagerness and examined the Scriptures every day to see if what Paul said was true. (Acts 17:11, NIV)

In Acts, we have the record of the Apostles preaching the Gospel in seven sermons given across the book – from Peter, to Stephen, to Paul. The Gospel was preached both to Jews and to Gentiles. And the Apostles were careful to say *certain things* about Jesus that would, to them, be the real Gospel that Jesus himself had sent them out with. So when we talk about the Gospel of Christ, we are referring to the message that preachers give the world at large about Jesus Christ; that is, *what has Jesus come to do?*

So, let's set up our own chart. Let's put the main points from the Apostles' sermons in the book of Acts in one column (or if you like, you can run through Acts and make your own list), and then write down the main points used in modern presentations of the Gospel in the second column.

The Apostles' Gospel	The Modern Gospel
· The Creator	· God loves you
· The Covenant with Abraham	· You are a sinner
· Moses and the Law	· Jesus died for you
· David's Kingdom	· Come to Jesus
· The Temple	· Believe and be saved
· The Prophets	· Accept Jesus as your Lord and Savior
· The Jews' Rejection of Christ	
· The Apostles' Testimony	
"If you do not believe that *I am the One I claim to be*, you will indeed die in your sins." (John 8:24)	Almost nothing said about Jesus; focuses mainly on the hearer's response

5

When we lay it all out in a chart like this, it's easy to see the difference between the two – they're not the same Gospel at all. Something happened in the Twentieth Century that caused the Church to drop the Apostolic Gospel and replace it with something else entirely new. And for some reason, everyone seems comfortable with that.

If nobody has ever compared these two versions of the Gospel before, it's either because it didn't occur to them or else because *they don't want to*. The first reason is simply due to ignorance, because it has never dawned on them the importance of the Apostles being our model for which Gospel to preach. The second reason is criminal in nature: preachers are deliberately avoiding the Apostles' message because of ulterior motives – and in our day, that means pleasing the public and maintaining their secure positions of power, respect, financial status and influence over the common laity.

Let's do it the way the Apostles showed us

Everything written in the New Testament was from the hands of the Apostles (or from men designated to speak for them). They were the ones to whom Christ revealed his Gospel; nobody else can claim that original contact with the Lord. And that means the Apostles are the *only* authority for the message of the Gospel.

And since this message was specifically for Christ's universal Church – his Bride – nobody has the right to change it in any way. The Apostles wouldn't have dared interfere in this private correspondence; their only duty was to faithfully deliver the message *as is*. If anybody changes the message, he has to take upon himself the responsibility for the resulting spiritual state of believers – and there isn't anybody who can bear that eternal burden, since we simply don't have the infinite wisdom necessary to answer for someone else's soul before God.

Like a recipe for a meal, or a formula for a scientific experiment, or a prescription for an illness, the Apostles' message was specially designed to address the spiritual condition of all humanity. Change it in any way, and the desired effect disappears. Unless one applies the proper truths, the soul will not conform to the image of Christ. In fact positively harmful things could happen if the message changes. This means that what the Apostles gave us is both necessary and sufficient – it will safely deliver us into God's presence just as Christ intended.

The Apostles knew that the leaders of the Church would also have to faithfully deliver the message unchanged to the flock – hence Paul's charge to the churches.

> Now I commend you because you remember me in everything and maintain the traditions even *as I delivered them to you.* (1 Corinthians 11:2)

> So then, brothers, stand firm and hold to the traditions *that you were taught by us*, either by our spoken word or by our letter. (2 Thessalonians 2:15)

In fact, Paul was aware that preachers tend to stray from the standards over time. So he issued a solemn curse – found in Galatians 1 – against anybody who would teach a Gospel different from the one he passed on to us (which we will look at shortly).

All this means that if we believe the same Gospel that the Apostles gave us, we then prove that we have inherited their treasure; we are *heirs* in a very real sense of our spiritual forefathers. We are not supposed to invent something new for our faith. We prove that we are children of our forefathers and part of the Family of Abraham when the world sees us holding onto the same truths that the Apostles held to.

If we don't believe the same Gospel, then we have no right to claim the name Christian, or to call our assemblies churches, or to call ourselves Bible-believing or Christ-centered. To make such claims, we have to show – as in a court of law – that we are committed to the same agenda that the Apostles followed.

Man-centered versus Christ-centered

There are two ways to present the Gospel: with Christ as the center, or with man as the center.

In our day, our consumerism and man-centered culture have changed the Church so much that we now approach everything in that light. We are mainly interested in what *we* are going to get out of the deal.

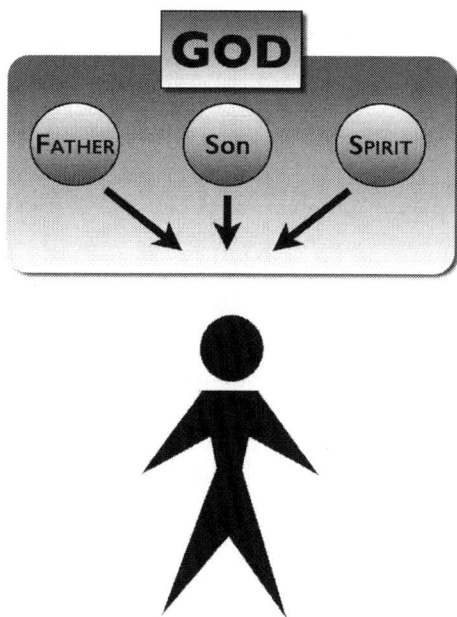

The "Fix" – Man is the center of activity

God (in the person of the Father, Son or Spirit – it really doesn't matter to us which one does the work, just push a button) does things to "fix" our personal circumstances. He saves us, blesses us, loves us, leads us, encourages us. The Gospel, indeed the whole of God's works on earth, is presented in this light.

Here again are the points that are used in the modern Gospel:

- God loves *you*.
- Jesus died for *you*.
- Repent and believe and *you* will be forgiven.
- Now *you* can go to Heaven.
- God will take care of *you*.

The whole emphasis of the message is on *you* – what you can have, what you will experience, what you do. Notice too that there is almost nothing said about what Jesus is and does – except for the fact that he "loves" us and he "died for us."

After we "accept" this message, we still have almost nothing to go on in our new faith. We're sitting there in church now, having accomplished what was expected of us, and now we don't know what to do with ourselves. It's as if we took just a single course in college to prepare for our career, and then we are brought in to assume our new position with only that little bit to go on. We're sitting there still clueless about what's going on, what our role is, what the company is all about, our relationships with others, etc. So it's no wonder that Christians come up with busywork to fill up the void in church – which is why people turn to legalism, eschatology, politics, community service, anything to make them feel useful. As if Church was all about *that*.

If all that we know about God is his "love," and if all that we're told about Christ is that he somehow "fixed" our problems, that pretty much narrows down our "faith" to about 1% of what the Bible deals with – if that much. We have no idea about what else Jesus might be doing and we really don't care, since it doesn't apply to our current personal situation.

But the Gospel is not so narrow and superficial. Because we aren't seeing the entire Mission, there are therefore huge areas of our lives that aren't being addressed at all. That means that people are still living independently of God – they are making their own decisions in life, they are setting their own values, they are creating their own world around them to suit themselves. Therefore God and the Bible actually play a minor role in the lives of those who claim to be "Christians."

Now let's look at a Christ-centered Gospel. The goal is to describe the entire program that Jesus came to do among men. The program (surprisingly enough) comes from the Old Testament, not the New Testament.

> … the *sacred writings*, which are able to make you wise for salvation through faith in Christ Jesus. (2 Timothy 3:15)

To Paul, the "sacred writings" were *the Old Testament*. He's saying plainly that we learn about salvation, we gain faith in Christ Jesus, by studying the Old Testament. In other words, the data for the Gospel is there in the Jewish Scriptures.

God first called Israel to be his Firstborn son (Exodus 4). Through their history he taught the world what the relationship really is between Father and Son – that is, between God and Christ Jesus.

THE FATHER PREPARES THE SON

New Creation

Covenant Heir

Deliverance & Law

Temple

Kingdom

Wisdom

Prophet

10

The Old Testament describes to us how the Father prepares his Firstborn son to live with him; it's a step-by-step program to bring him into the "fullness of the Son." The Good News – the Gospel – is that Jesus came to become one of us (he became the New Man), and to then take that New Man through the same OT program, this time successfully. It's the accomplishment of something that we were all meant to do, but only Jesus achieved. Now because of him a perfect Man lives in Heaven with the Father, and his Father is "pleased" with him.

> A voice from Heaven said, "This is my beloved Son, with whom I am well pleased." (Matthew 3:17)

And that means, of course, that now we also have hope for that same life with the Father – if we become "one with the Son."

With this Gospel, our agenda (in the Church and individually) has been expanded to eternity and infinity.

> And he gave the Apostles, the Prophets, the evangelists, the shepherds and teachers, to equip the saints for the work of ministry, for building up the body of Christ, until we all attain to the unity of the faith and of the knowledge of the Son of God, to mature manhood, to the measure of the stature of the fullness of Christ, so that we may no longer be children. (Ephesians 4:11-14)

Our goal for us now as Christians is to grow into the fullness of the Son of God.

To the Jew first

Not every human being will be saved. In fact, very few (relatively speaking) will see Heaven in the end. God made a decision a long time ago that this reward would only be for a select few – the "chosen" from among the nations. God, of course, reserved the right to choose whom he wanted to receive salvation, and he decided to start with the Jews.

11

For I am not ashamed of the Gospel, for it is the power of God for salvation to everyone who believes, *to the Jew first* and also to the Greek. (Romans 2:16)

This verse is not only describing what happened in the Gospel accounts. It's true that Jesus focused his ministry mainly on the Jews, and the Gentiles weren't added to the Church until later in the book of Acts. But there's more historical depth here than that: it's not just that *Jesus* went to the Jews first, but that *God* went to them first. The story starts with the Old Testament, not the New.

Turn back to Genesis 12 and you will read of God choosing the first Hebrew – Abraham, the father of the Jewish race – to be his heir. God swore to give Abraham and his descendants four Covenant promises, and all the Jews ever since then have cherished that Covenant as Family property, their inheritance from the Lord. For 2000 years they were the heirs of God while the rest of the world suffered and died in sin and darkness and hopelessness.

In fact, the bond that God made between himself and the Jews was the closest possible type – that of a Father and Son.

Thus says the LORD,

Israel is my Firstborn son. (Exodus 4:22)

That means that the story of the entire Old Testament is *the relationship of the Firstborn son with his Father*. *This* is how God raises his son; the data that explains God's Family life is all recorded there. So when Jesus came to the Jews, he wasn't telling them anything they didn't already know. In fact if he had, they would have justifiably rejected him outright – they didn't want any religion except the one that they had inherited from the Patriarchs.

Jesus' message to the Jews was this: he was there to lift up their special relationship with God from the physical to the spiritual level. Now they could take everything they had learned and apply it to God's world. Their physical system was done; he was leading them from the shadows into the Light. And he, being the Eternal Son whom they were all patterned after in their training, was the one who would take them there. He is the New Man, and their hope now was to be united with him forever as the Son of God. *That's* the "good news" that Jesus proclaimed to the Jews.

> Jesus came into Galilee, proclaiming the Gospel of God, and saying, "The time is fulfilled, and the Kingdom of God is at hand; repent and believe in the Gospel." (Mark 1:14-15)

As you can see, redemption – and being forgiven of one's sins – was only one aspect of the full picture of the Gospel. To preach a crippled Gospel that only has that one point is to miss the entire point.

The Gospel preached to the Gentiles *was no different.* The Apostle Paul states very clearly that even Gentiles are now descendants of Abraham. Through their faith, they are now heirs of the same inheritance that was offered to the Jews. That same OT program is now critical for *their* spiritual growth as sons of God.

> If you are Christ's, then you are Abraham's offspring, heirs according to promise. (Galatians 3:29)

If our "Gospel message" doesn't educate people about what we inherit from Abraham, or the Kingdom of David, or the Temple and priesthood, or the Prophetic message, then it's not the Gospel. Christianity isn't a different religion from the Jewish faith – it's the faith of the Jews lifted up to the spiritual world of God, point for point. Gentiles have been added into the Family of Abraham so that we now inherit those same promises made to him in the beginning.

> Some of the branches were broken off, and you, although a wild olive shoot, were grafted in among the others and now share in the nourishing root of the olive tree. (Romans 11:17)

The problem is – do Gentiles even know what they've inherited? They never will with today's truncated Gospel.

Following our culture

Modern America has pretty much closed the Bible in many ways. It's no wonder we don't know about our inheritance from our spiritual forefathers when sermons and lessons focus in such a narrow way on God's love and forgiveness and Christian living and receiving God's "blessings" in this world. Though the modern Church borrows many words and phrases from Scripture, it has put new meanings to those words that reflect our cultural man-centered focus.

Church – a million dollar investment

Church service – entertainment

Ministry – the clergy

Faith – devotion to whatever we believe

Righteousness – an outward appearance of goodness

Community of faith – one hour on Sunday

Family of faith – only those who go to our church

Scriptures – a few favorite passages in the NT or Psalms

The Gospel – get forgiveness so that we can go to Heaven

This is *not* what Christians in the First Century thought of when using these words. But then our generation has a fatal disdain for history, for learning from the past, and especially for comparing what we are doing with what past generations did. We consider them as primitive compared to ourselves with our modern achievements and "wisdom." So the modern Christian really doesn't care whether Paul had something else in mind when using these words. Practically speaking, then, we have eliminated the Bible and Church history from our worldview.

Hardly anybody in history has had life as good as the average American does now. Why would we take the past seriously when the here-and-now is so appealing? And that means, of course, that the original Gospel has to be *changed* to suit our present circumstances so as not to threaten our comfortable lifestyle.

What American culture has done is provided almost all of us with about 90% of what we want in life; and now that we're prosperous and comfortable, we can fill in the rest of what we need with a little religion at church. Our culture has produced *consumers*. All we want now from God is "icing on the cake" – a little soul-searching, a few encouraging words from Scripture, a hope for a future world after we're done here in this world. We certainly don't want any drastic, life-changing, bridge-burning demands that will threaten our prosperous and comfortable way of life.

And that means that certain aspects of the Biblical Gospel just don't fit in with our modern church life. The Gospel focuses on what Jesus is – the New Man – as he lives in Heaven now, *not* on what we want from God in this world. It focuses on preparation for a new life with God, *not* getting more comfortable in this life. It focuses on spiritual realities, *not* the entertainments and comforts that our culture gives us. The true Gospel takes us out of this world and puts us in front of the throne of God.

Since the "Gospel" that we modern Christians want to hear, then, has been changed to reflect the culture that we're so in love with, and since we already have most of what we want in life (we wouldn't think of giving any of it up, not even for God!), all we want from God is just that little 10% that we still need to make life more fulfilling in some way.

The message is not "God loves you!"

The Gospel that we now hear consists of a universal message: *God loves you*. It's the core of every evangelistic sermon, in almost every kind of church and ministry across America. Never mind the fact that the Apostles never preached this in their Gospel messages; that's what *we* want to hear.

The idea is that God feels sorry for you, so he's going to help you out. You have to do something first about the fact that you're a sinner; but once you receive forgiveness, you can put that nasty business behind you (Jesus will take care of all that for you) and start making plans on going to Heaven after this life. In the meantime, he can give you a lot of helps and "blessings" to make your life here in this world more comfortable and enjoyable. And don't worry about cutting your ties with the world – you can be a Christian and enjoy our modern American "blessings" too. (So the sermons that condemn the "world" never do get very specific concerning what they mean by "world" – because that might threaten what we love and claim as our "rights" as Americans.)

Here's a typical presentation of the modern Gospel, taken from a ministry on the Internet.

> *We have all sinned and deserve God's judgment. God, the Father, sent His only Son to satisfy that judgment for those who believe in Him. Jesus, the creator and eternal Son of God, who lived a sinless life, loves us so much that He died for our sins, taking the punishment that we deserve, was buried, and rose from the dead according to the Bible. If you truly believe and trust this in your heart, receiving Jesus alone as your Savior, declaring, "Jesus is Lord," you will be saved from judgment and spend eternity with God in heaven.*[1]

Unfortunately this "Gospel" actually tells us almost nothing about God according to the Bible.

- **Sinned** – We must have done something that God doesn't like, but what it was we aren't told.

---

[1] *http://www.allaboutgod.com/what-is-sin.htm*

- **Satisfy that judgment** –As if this is *all* that Jesus did! That was only one of many crucial steps in his agenda, all of which are necessary for God's children and their faith.

- **Loves us** – What kind of love? There are all kinds, including a love for his Creation, his angels, a love that allows the creature to enjoy his blessings. Is it just an emotional feeling on his part – a "love" that gives us a warm feeling that someone cares about us? Who wouldn't want that!

- **Lived a sinless life** – Again, this covers only a single phase of what Jesus accomplished – and doesn't tell us why he did it.

- **Rose from the dead** – There's no information here about why he rose from the dead, how it happened, where he is now, what he's doing now, why he left, or what state he's in now. As if he simply disappeared from view, and now we go back to our lives here in this world. We're impressed, but there's nothing useable here.

- **Truly believe** – Believe what? No data is given here except "Jesus died for our sins." That's the same as saying "Joe Smith died for his country." Where does that put us? What difference does it make? There's just hardly anything to go on here.

- **Jesus is Lord** – Why was that important to God that Jesus becomes "Lord"? What does "Lord" mean to God? What does that mean in an American's life, Christian though he/she be?

- **Spend eternity with God** – So do the angels. How will we be different? *Will* we be different? If so, in what way?

In short, this "Gospel" is extremely subjective, emotional, and short on details. The emphasis is on *you*, the listener. The message is that you are missing a few things in God's eyes, and so God and Jesus came to "fix" you and give you something great in the end. At no point does this Gospel refer to anything from the Old Testament; and in no way does it reflect what Jesus came to do. Instead it uses modern cultural values to satisfy the consumer and appeal to his emotions. The whole Gospel has been stripped down to something almost useless, that has no resemblance at all to the Gospel preached by the Apostles. If we boil it all down to just the bare bones, this Gospel essentially says that –

- *God loves you.*

- *Jesus is going to take care of your sin problem.*

- *You're going to love it in Heaven.*

Based on this extremely limited picture, what will people think they're accepting? Only that someone cares about them, and that things will turn out all right in the end if they agree to play the game. Even then, people don't really learn the point of the game nor how it's played.

That is *not* the Gospel of Christ. The Apostles didn't preach this kind of Gospel, nor did the historic Church. This is purely a modern invention of a spiritually bankrupt generation.

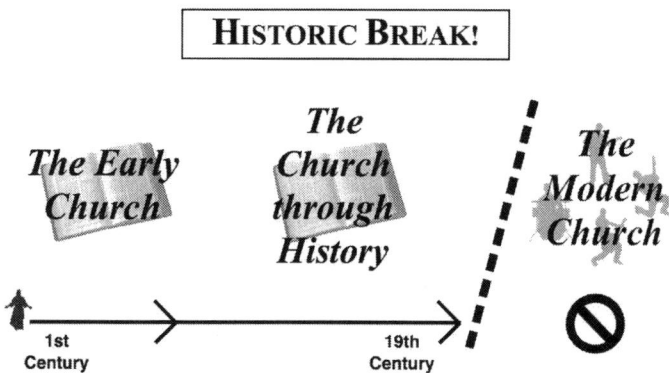

HISTORIC BREAK!

The Early Church

The Church through History

The Modern Church

1st Century   19th Century

18

I have never been able to understand the strange logic of modern preachers when they assure everyone right up front that God loves them. The Bible says no such thing. With one breath they claim that "God loves you!" Then in the next breath they say "And if you don't believe in Jesus he will throw you into Hell!" Any thinking person can see through that nonsense, and of course they won't trust a ministry that teaches it; it sounds suspiciously manipulative. The truth is that God *loves* the world that he made. (Genesis 1:31; John 3:16) But God *hates* the "world" that man and the devil replaced it with. (1 John 2:15-17) God *loves* his children. (John 14:21) But God *hates* the wicked. (Psalm 11:5) God is *merciful* to those who repent. (Exodus 34:6-7) But God will *punish* those who do not repent. (Genesis 34:7) Let's just stick with what the Bible *says*, instead of what we want it to say. When we change the message, we have created a false Gospel. And usually, when people change the message of Scripture, they have an ulterior motive.

The problem is not so much what the new Gospel is telling us, but rather what it's *not* telling us.

- It's not telling us why God would take a Father/Son approach to us.

- It's telling us hardly anything about who Jesus is, or what he did.

- It's not telling us what this love of God consists of, or how it works.

- It's not telling us what to believe – just that we have to believe.

- It's not telling us what our hope really is.

And yet, for as disappointing as this kind of Gospel actually is, you will hear it everywhere from almost every pulpit in our generation. Even with those who claim to be more careful about how to understand the message of the Bible, this is the only Gospel you will hear from them. Something happened at the turn of the Twentieth Century to cause the Church to turn away to another Gospel.

Disaster looms

In the Bible, a key part of the message was always the "good news" that if people acted *now*, they could escape the disaster that was looming over their heads.

For example, when Jesus preached to the Jews, it was under the looming threat of God's wrath about to break out against them. He lived about 30 AD; just forty years later – in 70 AD – the Romans would overwhelm Jerusalem and destroy it completely and scatter the survivors all over the world. The entire physical system of the Jewish religion was about to be torn apart and thrown away for good. It was the most traumatic moment in their 2000-year history. The Messiah was actually giving them a "last chance" to turn back to God before he unleashed his fury against his own people for their obstinate unbelief and immorality. (Luke 21:22-24)

The Gospel has always had this same urgency to it. Noah was a "preacher of righteousness" who, by his actions of faith, testified in his generation of the reality of God. While everyone was "eating and drinking and marrying and giving in marriage," suddenly without warning the Lord destroyed the entire earth with all of its inhabitants. Only eight were saved in the Flood of God's wrath.

The "good news" preached to the Israelites bound in slavery in Egypt was that their God was going to deliver them from their bondage in an awesome display of power. So while he was bringing them out, he also dealt Egypt a crippling blow with ten plagues, and then sent her army to the bottom of the Red Sea. Israel was saved in the midst of one of the most ferocious displays in history of the wrath of God against his enemies.

Isaiah (and other prophets) preached "good news" to a generation of hard-hearted Israelites – that they still had time to come back to God and repent of their sins and escape the coming wrath. They didn't listen. So God's people were slaughtered by the thousands, and the survivors were dragged off to Babylon for seventy years of captivity among the pagans. They ignored the urgency of the message.

The Apostle Peter preached his first Gospel message to the Jews, warning them of the same kind of disaster. "Save yourselves from this crooked generation." (Acts 2:40) What they didn't know, and what he could see coming, was that final judgment of God against the old Jewish system that would destroy their entire way of life in just a generation's time. They were, in Peter's sermon, seeing the last door opening for their salvation and giving them a way out before it was too late. (Luke 19:43-44)

But Peter saw an even greater disaster on the horizon: the destruction of the whole world. It wouldn't be another Flood, but something worse – "By the same Word the heavens and earth that now exist are stored up for fire, being kept until the day of judgment and destruction of the ungodly." (2 Peter 3:7) And the Gospel? "According to his promise we are waiting for new heavens and a new earth in which righteousness dwells." (2 Peter 3:13) There is a way out for the righteous.

An essential element of the Gospel, therefore, is revealing the danger that people are in. Far from the Heavenly love letter that modern preachers turn it into, the message is that we are all dead. We are "without hope and without God." We fully deserve what's coming for us. The only ones who will "escape the wrath to come" will be those who can see the Light who has come from Heaven, who is calling his sheep to come to him to be taken out of this world, into the Father's presence for a new Life with him.

Good news

Now let's lay out the true Gospel and see it in full contrast to the false Gospel.

The false Gospel teaches that man is in trouble with God, but that Jesus can take care of the problem – and then, after peace is made with God, man can go to Heaven after this life is over. The trouble with this Gospel is not in what it says, but what in it *doesn't* say. And the result is that people will make some small changes in their lives, and then sit back contented, with a clean conscience, enjoying "church," and waiting for the next world. That's all it amounts to – just a ticket into Heaven.

The true Gospel, on the other hand, is an enormous concept with radical consequences for one's life – both now and in the future. It draws principles directly from the Old Testament that teach us how God prepared his Firstborn son for a special life with him. The Jews were thoroughly familiar with these principles; what most of them didn't realize, however, was that God never intended for his children to be limited by this physical world. It's all about God's world. The task here is to change us into the image of the Son for whom all things were made.

Preachers act as if being forgiven and justified by Christ's death was the end-all of God's works among us. It was not. It was the means to the end. Justification gets us to the door of the Temple; it's true that we'll never get in unless we are perfectly righteous. But now we need to go inside God's House and live the special life of the Firstborn Son with our Father. *That's* what the Gospel is about; Jesus has made it possible for us to do that.

> And those whom he predestined he also called, and
> those whom he called he also justified, and those whom
> he justified he also *glorified*. (Romans 8:30)

The purpose of Jesus' coming was to show us the Eternal Son of God, in his full glory, revealing the depth of his life with the Father *in Heaven*. And when he in himself joined God and man together, that was the staggering new aspect of the Gospel that the Apostles taught us: now *we* can be part of the Family of God just as Jesus is. Man is now elevated to the level of the Son of God.

To the faithful Jews this was exciting news. Jesus accomplished what 2000 years of Jewish efforts could not do, not even on the physical level. Those who could see the spiritual world of God (beyond this world) realized the amazing work that Christ did for them. To them, this was indeed *good news*.

The lessons are all from the Old Testament, but now Jesus reveals to us the same concepts as they exist in Heaven in his relationship with the Father.

- Man – in Christ – is now **re-created** so that he can know God as he is, so that he can live in God's world. His new body is joined with the resurrected Son of God and brought into the world of God.

- Man is now the **Heir** of the fullness of God. Everything that God is and has now belongs to man.

- Man is now made **Holy** – or God-centered – so that, cleansed of all unrighteousness, clothed with the righteousness of the Son himself, he can know and receive the fullness of the depths of God.

- Man now has **full access** to God as a Son – nothing in God is withheld from him. The Father calls his Son into his presence to live with him forever as Family.

- Man now sits at God's right hand and **rules** God's Kingdom, under God, using God's agenda, passionate about God's glory, with all God's authority and power.

- Man now knows the **mind** of God, he is filled with the wisdom of God; the Son learns directly from the Father and therefore sees all things as the Father does.

- Man is now God's **spokesman** because he is "the image of his Father" in all ways. God now reveals himself through man.

So the Son has gone back to the Father and his life of glory – but now as the God/man. Jesus has put man in the Trinity Family relationship in himself.

- In order to do this, he first had to destroy the barriers that kept man from this kind of life: sin and death. So he became one of us, and then put man (as he is now) to death. "Flesh and blood cannot inherit the Kingdom of God, nor does the perishable inherit the imperishable." (1 Corinthians 15:50) Unfortunately this is the best that modern preachers can do; they generally stop at this point of the message.

- But the next step was crucial: he then raised this dead man "into newness of life" and became a New Man, fully capable and ready to return to his Father and their unique relationship. The Ascension is just as critical to the Gospel as the Resurrection.

- The final step involves us directly: Christ sent his Spirit into us who are God's children to join us with him, to become his Body, so that now the life he lives with his Father, we all live. "For you have died, and your life is hidden with Christ in God." (Colossians 3:3)

This isn't just a place allotted for us in Heaven – as any angel might expect to receive. This is a place within the Trinity Family life; as Peter described it – "… so that … you may become partakers of the divine nature." (2 Peter 1:4) We are truly "with Christ in God." This guarantees that whatever Christ experiences, we also experience. Nothing less.

GOD

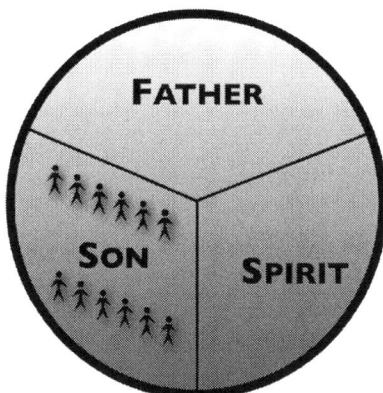

This is the Gospel of the Apostles.

The Preaching of the Gospel

There remains, of course, the announcement of the Gospel – which is where preaching comes in.

Paul refers to those who "preach the good news" (Romans 10:15), which is a quote from the Prophet Isaiah.

How beautiful upon the mountains

    are the feet of him who brings good news,

    who publishes peace, who brings good news of happiness,

    who publishes salvation,

    who says to Zion, "Your God reigns."

The voice of your watchmen – they lift up their voice;

    together they sing for joy;

    for eye to eye they see

    the return of the LORD to Zion. (Isaiah 52:7-8)

25

To the Jews this would have been fabulous news. Isaiah was looking into their future as captives in Babylon; in their exile they were destitute and without God. They had lost everything – the Temple, the sacrifices, their homes, Jerusalem itself, the Kingdom, the Covenant Promises. But when someone appeared with the news of "the return of the LORD to Zion," they were overjoyed. This is what they wanted to hear! The Lord was going to rebuild their city and restore their national treasures to them. For man this was impossible; but the power of God was about to do the impossible for them. So he took them back home to Jerusalem amid great celebrations.

Now we have Jesus, who was sent to the lowest regions of the earth, and in himself destroyed sinful man, who was then raised from the dead a New Man. And then ... "the LORD returned to Zion." This God/Man *ascended* to the Heavenly Jerusalem where he ...

> ... is seated at the right hand of the throne of the Majesty in Heaven. (Hebrews 8:1)

And for those who understand, this is "good news!" Christ is now preparing a new eternal Creation, a new City, a new House of God, a new Inheritance according to the Abrahamic Covenant, a new Kingdom patterned after David's, a new Priesthood – everything that the Jews had hoped for, but now on a spiritual, eternal level. This is the life of the mature Son in the presence of God himself.

This good news creates faith and hope in the hearts of all those who have been "chosen in him before the foundation of the world." (Ephesians 1:4) It's *that* life that the true believer wants to be part of. Hearing about it draws them to the Christ. They are longing for the day that they too can "go home."

> In my Father's house are many rooms. If it were not so, would I have told you that I go to prepare a place for you? And if I go and prepare a place for you, I will come

again and will take you to myself, that where I am you may be also. (John 14:2-3)

That which we have seen and heard we proclaim also to you, so that you too may have fellowship with us; and indeed our fellowship is with the Father and with his Son Jesus Christ. (1 John 1:3)

And when the Gentiles heard this, they began rejoicing and glorifying the Word of the Lord, and as many as were appointed to eternal life believed. (Acts 13:48)

A false gospel

The Apostle Paul issued a serious warning to preachers and teachers about the Gospel and how to present it – and even for those who hear and believe it.

I am astonished that you are so quickly deserting him who called you in the grace of Christ and are turning to a different Gospel — not that there is another one, but there are some who trouble you and want to distort the Gospel of Christ. But even if we or an angel from Heaven should preach to you a Gospel contrary to the one we preached to you, *let him be accursed*. As we have said before, so now I say again: If anyone is preaching to you a Gospel contrary to the one you received, *let him be accursed*. (Galatians 1:6-9)

Listen to Paul's warning. The Gospel isn't just about being forgiven and going to Heaven. It's about the fullness of the Son of God, the return of the God/Man Jesus Christ to Mt. Zion, and sharing in his life with the Father. If we don't focus on the Point, or if we leave any of the critical details out, or we add or emphasize our favorite themes in order to achieve our own purposes, then we're distorting the message. We will be cheating the children of their bread and misleading the unbelievers. We will be guilty of withholding the inheritance from the heirs, and of giving false hope to sinners who have no intention of changing their lives to conform to God's expectations.

Of course it takes a great deal of study of the Scriptures to grasp the Mission of the Son of God. Paul himself spent years getting re-programmed on the real meaning of the Old Testament to counteract the misinformation he had received in his Pharisaic training. But if someone doesn't know how to preach the Gospel the way the Apostles did it, then they need to sit down and let someone else do it, in light of this condemnation in Galatians. It's safer to keep quiet than to tell lies. "Not many of you should presume to be teachers, my brothers, because you know that we who teach will be judged more strictly." (James 3:1)

In Paul's mind, what would be a Gospel "contrary to the one he preached"? In order to answer this question, you have to do a serious study of the Gospel as he presents it in his Letters – for example, in Romans. "I am eager to preach the Gospel to you also who are in Rome." (Romans 1:15) You have to make careful notes on the subjects he covers, the data he uses to present the message of Christ, the way he handles the concepts. Without going into such an extensive study here, we can note a few of the subjects he covers:

- He uses the Old Testament deeply and extensively.

- He gives us a clear picture of God in his wrath and his mercy.

- He paints a dismal picture of man without God – and of wrath awaiting the sinner. As we are now, we are useless to God and deserving of death.

- He tells us a great deal about the Son of God, and what he has done.

- He shows us that salvation rests in union with the Son.

28

- He proclaims that our hope is a new life as the Son of God.

So a false Gospel would look more like this:

- Very little data from the Old Testament.
- A different God from what the Bible presents to us.
- An encouraging picture of man – only a very few changes need to be made.
- Almost nothing about who Jesus is.
- Salvation is simply being forgiven and justified.
- Our hope is that the loving God will take care of us.

You may not have gone through the exercise of comparing the Gospel that is preached now in our day against what the Apostles preached, but it is definitely worth doing. Usually we *assume* that what we're doing is right, and yet we make *no effort at all* to compare the actual data. That's willful blindness. In light of our sinful nature, and our inherent weakness, and our natural ignorance of the ways and works of God, the responsible thing to do is to keep checking to see if we're still on the right road.

> Examine yourselves, to see whether you are in the faith. Test yourselves. Or do you not realize this about yourselves, that Jesus Christ is in you? — unless indeed you fail to meet the test! (2 Corinthians 13:5)

If we preach something different from the Apostles' Gospel then we aren't delivering to the children of God what the Father wants them to hear.

> "Woe to the shepherds who destroy and scatter the sheep of my pasture!" declares the LORD. Therefore thus says the LORD, the God of Israel, concerning the shepherds who care for my people: "You have scattered my flock and have driven them away, and you have not attended to them. Behold, I will attend to you for your evil deeds, declares the LORD. Then I will gather the

remnant of my flock out of all the countries where I have driven them, and I will bring them back to their fold, and they shall be fruitful and multiply. I will set shepherds over them who will care for them, and they shall fear no more, nor be dismayed, neither shall any be missing, declares the LORD." (Jeremiah 23:1-4)

And now?

It makes a great deal of difference which Gospel someone preaches. If it's a false Gospel, then we end up with a very low-level religion. There isn't much for you to take care of: simply get forgiveness and pick up your ticket to Heaven. In the meantime you need to come to church, sit back and enjoy the show, and do and say a few key things that let people know that you're part of the club now. And you can still enjoy our rich American culture by calling it the Lord's "blessings" – there's actually very little about your life that you need to change or get rid of, just some of the more obvious gross sins.

Hopefully you can see that this in no way resembles the Gospel that the Apostles preached. Read the book of Acts to see how drastically the lives of the believers changed when they heard the Gospel. They became a Body, and began training for the life of the Son. They were ostracized by their culture, and put to death for their faith – and went to the flames cheerfully. And that was because their hope was not for this world, but the next; not just a promise of eternal life in Heaven, but of union with the Son of God. *Jesus went back to the Father* – and that's the good news that so attracted them. In him they were moving from the bottom rung of this world to the right hand of the throne of God.

They could also see the end approaching, and there was little enough time to get ready for such a staggering role that God had planned for them. Every minute counted. In the end, God gives his rewards only to those who do as Paul did. "Forgetting what lies behind and straining forward to what lies ahead, I press on toward the goal for the prize of the upward call of God in Christ Jesus." (Philippians 3:13-14)

> The one who conquers will have this heritage, and I will be his God and he will be my Son. (Revelation 21:7)

The son of the King shows his true character when he aims for this high goal.

Books available from
Ravenbrook Publishers

The Failure of the Modern American Church   *(150 pages)*

For the last 100 years, the Church in America has gradually changed, generation after generation, until it has lost its historic roots and has completely taken on the consumerism and media-driven character of modern American culture – with all its emptiness and banality.

The result is that the Church no longer has a voice in our culture, and America has lost its sole witness to the Truth. Continuing along the path that we're taking now will only make things worse. Our sins are finally catching up with us.

The only options left are either to go down with our culture in flames, or to pull back and reorganize along Biblical principles. It's going to mean walking away from our culture ("Carry the cross!") and re-establishing our Church life firmly on the Apostolic and Prophetic testimony. It's not likely that we will save America, but we may be able to bring the Church back to its Biblical roots – if we take drastic action now, before it's too late.

Mystery Revealed: A Beginner's Bible Survey   *(424 pages)*

This Survey takes the student through the entire Bible – first with an analysis of the whole Bible, then looking at the major divisions of the Bible and how they contribute to the whole picture.

Eight Fundamentals of the Christian Faith   *(361 pages)*

According to Hebrews, each believer should be thoroughly familiar with the basics of the faith, so much so that you can teach others. This is an in-depth study of each of the basics mentioned in Hebrews.

Jesus and the New Testament   *(349 pages)*

The New Testament is made up of two things: the story of Jesus' life on earth, and the Apostles' testimony of his unique nature and work. The result is a living fulfillment of God's project of salvation that was first worked out in the Old Testament.

Where the Paths Meet   *(269 pages)*

This book focuses on the major aspects of both Old and New Testaments to show how the entire Bible forms one story, one way of salvation, one road to God.

Ten Keys to the Bible   *(591 pages)*

There are certain "keys" that the student needs to learn for studying the Bible. Master these Keys, and you will be better equipped to unlock any passage of the Bible and find its true meaning.

The Witness   *(258 pages)*

God wisely arranged the Bible as a collection of affidavits of eyewitnesses who can testify to the reality and works of God. These witnesses have given us a written record of God that makes the Bible a bastion of truth that gives comfort to the saints and gives the church the foundation it needs to stand against attacks from the Enemy.

The Works of the Lord   *(345 pages)*

There are certain works that only God can do. The first order of business for every Christian is to find out what God's works are – not only to give us the agenda for our prayers, but also to teach us what to wait for. In wisdom we won't try to do God's works, but we will wait on God for what only he can do.

The Church Militant   *(194 pages)*

The Church has a Mission: God's people are called to prepare to live with him in Heaven. The problem is that there is going to be war for the people of God, all the way to the Promised Land. The military understands the concepts of a Mission, drills and training, discipline, unity, perseverance and loyalty. The purpose of this book is to transfer the concepts of military discipline and fighting to the context of the Church, and equip the leaders to achieve their objective.

A Bible Catechism   *(146 pages)*

One of the best ways to learn the major doctrines of our faith is by question and answer. This book teaches the student about the basics of

Christianity through easy-to-understand answers to questions that even children can understand.

The Bible Explains Creation *(293 pages)*

The Bible gives us a fuller description of how God created the universe than science can ever give us. But you have to use the entire Bible, from Genesis to Revelation, to see the spiritual framework that supports our physical world.

Glory: The Holiness of God and Man *(122 pages)*

Man was created to know and enjoy God – this is the definition of holiness. Sin separated us from God; so the work of Christ is to restore that relationship and lift man up to a higher level than we thought imaginable – to know God *as Jesus knows him*.

A Holy Temple *(198 pages)*

The church was designed to be a formidable force in our society; unfortunately in our day it's become weak and ineffective. This book explores a number of areas that will strengthen the testimony and work of a church to give it the truth and power that modern man needs.

Knots Untied *(229 pages)*

There are certain issues in the Bible that, on the surface, look simple enough to understand – until you begin asking some probing questions. **Knots Untied** examines a few of these issues and finds some surprising answers.

The Measure of a Christian *(247 pages)*

The Measure of a Christian looks at the root issues of living the Christian life. What are the marks of a true Christian? What kind of church does a Christian need to grow spiritually? How important is discipline to a person's life? How does God discipline his children?

A New Model for Biblical Studies *(59 pages)*

The traditional way of looking at the Bible, unfortunately, has robbed us of its richness and usability. In this book we take a slightly different approach and find not only the treasure chest of the Old Testament opening up to us, but a clear picture of how it unfolds into the New Testament.

No Proof Needed   *(83 pages)*

Men and nations have attacked the Bible for thousands of years, but it still reveals the truth about God and man in spite of the attacks. If we understand the wisdom behind the making of the Bible, we will see that God doesn't need our efforts to prove its truth – it stands on its own.

The Secret to Answered Prayer   *(188 pages)*

The Bible is very specific about how one must approach God. In this book we learn six principles to keep in mind if one wants answers from the God of the Bible.

Profitable Servants   *(113 pages)*

Jesus taught about the "unprofitable servant" to impress on us the many duties that he holds us all responsible for. Even one talent is more than you might think! This book explores the responsibilities that the Lord has given his people.

Teaching Children About Jesus   *(324 pages)*

Children will believe anything you teach them. That's why it's vitally important to get as much of the truth into their heads as you can while they are still open to it. Here we look at what you must teach about Jesus, and the message of the Bible, to lay a good foundation for their future.

The Throne of David   *(159 pages)*

David pulled the nation of Israel together according to a five-point plan, around a Mission that brought the people back to God. Jesus, as the Son of David, builds his church according to the same plan. We need to learn that plan so that we can work with him, not against him, in our churches.

Tools for Bible Teachers   *(79 pages)*

Being a Bible teacher requires some important skills and resources; not every volunteer in church can do the job as God requires. This is an overview of what those skills are; with them, you can successfully teach the Bible to your students.

The *Treasury of Christ* Commentary of the Bible

This commentary focuses on bringing out the important points that a Christian needs for his spiritual faith and walk with God, book by book.

Completed volumes:

Volume 1: Overview of the Old Testament (190 pages)

Check with Ravenbrook for additional titles.

Removing the Veil   *(151 pages)*

Moses had to put a covering over his head to hide the Glory of God, which symbolized the fact that the Jews didn't understand the spiritual meanings behind the elements of their religion. Jesus removes that veil for Christians. This book explores the main themes of the Old Testament in an easy-to-read presentation, so that the Christian can understand why the Old Testament is so crucial for one's faith.

Words of Gold   *(187 pages)*

Many Christians have never been taught how to study the Bible. Here the student is introduced to the tools of Bible study, with numerous examples and homework.

A Manual for Spiritual Survival   *(203 pages)*

The modern church is in more of an entertainment mode than set up for training. But hard times will come upon every one of us, in some form. In this book we look at specific areas, for both the church and the individual Christian, to help them become survivors and to prepare for hardship and trial.

The Ways of the Lord   *(199 pages)*

The entire Bible teaches us that the Lord has ways of doing things. In Hebrews we read that the Israelites failed to learn those ways – which is why God refused to let them into the Promised Land. Christians also need to learn his ways if they want to enter Heaven.

What the Bible Says About Hell   *(100 pages)*

Hell is not what many people think it is. Here we learn exactly what Hell is like, and who will go there. Also covered are the many myths of

Hell that confuse so many people, and what the Bible really says about these issues.

Heirs of the Covenant   *(49 pages)*

This book explores two fundamental concepts of the Bible – the Abrahamic Covenant, and the shadow-to-reality switch from Old to New Testaments. These principles make the issue of baptism clear, and shows parents whether they can count their children as heirs of the Covenant in Christ before conversion.

The Jews: A Christian Perspective   *(156 pages)*

The Jews share our Scriptures, our God, our hope of Heaven – but they can't bring themselves to share our Messiah. The Jews have lost almost everything that used to make them unique in God's eyes. All they have now is a man-made religion that can't fulfill the commands of the Law of Moses. It's time for them to see that only in Christ will the Jew find what he is looking for in his God.

Preaching Christ   *(394 pages)*

A rich resource for pastors and teachers! Here in one volume is a comprehensive and illuminating study of what the entire Bible has to say about Jesus Christ:

- Turn moralisms into lessons on Christ
- Keys that unlock any passage to see God
- The Old Testament foundation for the New
- Seeing Jesus in the most difficult passages
- From Genesis to Revelation – for years of sermons and lessons on Christ!

Biblical Theology for Pastors & Teachers   *(Two Volumes, 700 pages)*

Here is a Biblical Theology for the Pastor/Teacher which provides the fundamental lessons of the Bible in a way that he can pass the doctrine of our Christian faith on to the church - in an easy-to-read, easy-on-the-eyes format. The overarching theme of the Bible is the Father/Son relationship. In fact, the entire Bible is a full description of this relationship between Father and Son, as God wants to see it in us. We know this because of the testimony of the best authority in the Bible – Jesus himself, the eternal Son of God. The reason he came was to gather a Family together and make them one with himself, in his image, so that they might become Sons of God. Using Christ and the

Apostles as the central hermeneutical principle, this theology pulls both Old and New Testaments together to form a whole picture of the message of the entire Bible.

Father and Son   *(120 pages)*

Here is the central message of the entire Bible. God first made man "in his image" – he created us as his Family on earth, with privileges as his children. Since man failed in that relationship, God is now creating a new Man who will live with the Father in Heaven. Through Israel's history we learn what it takes to create the new sons of God, and in the New Testament we see the eternal Son himself, with whom we are united in the Spirit to share his life in the Family of the Trinity. At the end of time, the process will be complete, and all those who are in Christ will be transformed into the image of the Son that God loves.

Before the Throne of God   *(150 pages)*

When the Lord sent Moses into Egypt to confront Pharaoh and bring his people out of slavery, he called Israel "My Firstborn Son."

Hidden in an obscure passage in the book of Numbers lies a minor historical event that later proved to be of tremendous spiritual consequence for the life of Israel.

The direct correlation of the Levites with the firstborn sons of Israel in Numbers 3 meant that their God planned to bring the Heirs of Abraham into such close fellowship with him as only exists between a Father and his Son.

The Fullness of the Son   *(142 pages)*

Church has taken many forms over the centuries. But always, Christ's true Church has been some form of the model set down for us in the time of the New Testament by the Apostles.

In order to understand what happens in Christ's Church, however, we have to put both Old and New Testaments together to form the complete picture: it's the growth of the spiritual Son being prepared to live with his Father in Heaven.

And God placed all things under his feet and appointed him to be head over everything for the Church, which is his Body, the fullness of him who fills everything in every way. (Ephesians 1:22-23)

You can order these books from Amazon on-line through these websites:

www.ravenbrook.org

www.shenbible.org

Manufactured by Amazon.ca
Bolton, ON

46384905R00024